IMAGES
of America

MISSIONS OF MONTEREY

The Mission of St. Carlos Near Monterey is a drawing of the second settlement in Carmel and the first dwellings, with Mission San Carlos Borromeo del Río Carmelo at the left. The early mission courtyard was dominated by the cross raised by Fr. Junípero Serra. By 1789, the first chapel, built of logs, and many other buildings were consumed in a fire and later replaced. The sketch is by John Sykes, who arrived with British explorer Capt. George Vancouver aboard the *Daedalus* in 1792. (Library of Congress, Historic American Buildings Survey/Historic American Engineering Record/Historic American Landscapes Survey.)

On the Cover: Mission San Carlos Borromeo del Rio Carmelo is pictured after the first modern restoration in 1924, a replacement that changed the authentic slope, materials, and pitch later corrected in 1936. This original photograph was recently discovered with nearly 100 glass plates on California's missions from around 1928 to 1938. In 1961, Mission San Carlos Borromeo del Rio Carmelo was dedicated as a basilica, one of just over 300 in America. (Author's collection.)

IMAGES
of America

MISSIONS OF MONTEREY

Robert A. Bellezza

ARCADIA
PUBLISHING

ISBN 978-0-7385-9682-2

Published by Arcadia Publishing
Charleston, South Carolina

Library of Congress Control Number: 2012941994

For all general information, please contact Arcadia Publishing:
Telephone 843-853-2070
Fax 843-853-0044
E-mail sales@arcadiapublishing.com
For customer service and orders:
Toll-Free 1-888-313-2665

Visit us on the Internet at www.arcadiapublishing.com

To my granddaughters Rachel and Rebecca and all California history readers who find a spark of the past may inspire any dream in their hearts.

Contents

Acknowledgments

The Library of Congress Prints & Photographs Online Collection has supplied the majority of images within this volume and makes possible a review of California's founding architectural landmarks practically lost through centuries of age, deterioration, and neglect. California's mission buildings were rescued only after the majority had suffered irreversible weathering and ruin to the adobe walls. The work employing the Civilian Conservation Corps (CCC) and photographers from the 1933 New Deal documented the progress or decay of the many iconic structures through the Historic American Building Survey. Unless otherwise indicated, all images are courtesy of the Library of Congress, Historic American Buildings Survey/Historic American Engineering Record/Historic American Landscapes Survey. By the beginning of the 20th century, several organizations—including the Landmarks Club program, headed by Charles F. Lummis, which evolved into the California Historical Landmarks League, led by Joseph R. Knowland—had begun preserving the earliest missions, often built and decorated entirely by California natives. Several photographs within this volume are released for the first time from the author's collection or from the Anderson family's collection of vintage glass plates. Select images in the author's collection were located by Rhys Yeakley are noted as magic lantern slides made by the Charles Beseler Co. in or after 1905. My deepest appreciation goes to a good friend in Monterey, Richard Quaglia, a hospitality business owner whose help greatly opened my knowledge of the area. Many up-to-date mission photographs featured in "Missions Past & Present: Touring El Camino Real" are from my visits to the Monterey area and my association in media over 10 years with Richard. Also, many thanks are given to Dennis Copeland, Museums, Cultural Arts and Archives manager at the California History Room, for using the photographic archive and his keen eye for historical details of the subject; and to Jerry Hornor, historian at San Carlos Cathedral Museum. Special appreciation is given to Amy Perryman, associate publisher at Arcadia Publishing, for her guidance through the process and believing we could make it possible.

We are truly pleased our book's release coincides with the 300th anniversary year of Fr. Junípero Serra's birth. His name was Miguel Josep Serra (Junípero was his chosen religious name), born November 24, 1713, in Petra, Majorca, one of the Balearic Islands, located some 150 miles off the coast of the Spanish mainland.

Introduction

Sighting from the Sea

Spain's monumental task building missions throughout the New World would leave an indelible mark on the history of California. This became especially true in Monterey, the historical capital of Alta California and the second military presidio established by Spain's viceroy general in Mexico City. Seafaring explorers claimed Alta California's unexplored shores for the Spanish Crown as early as 1542, after Portuguese navigator Juan Rodriguez Cabrillo discovered its shoreline. Sighting of Monterey's harbor by another Portuguese sailor, Sebastián Rodriguez Cermeño, was made in 1595. Cermeño passed through Monterey's port in a makeshift boat he salvaged to save his crew on retreat to Mexico after his galleon broke up on the rocky shores where Sir Francis Drake had landed successfully 16 years earlier. Sailing under instructions of Spain's Philip III in 1602, successful Spanish merchant Don Sebastián Vizcaíno was the first navigator to enter Monterey's pristine port. His explorations charted Point Pinos on the coast and sailed into the serene waters of Monterey Bay, where he made landfall under the spreading branches of an oak tree. Accompanied by three Carmelite fathers performing singing mass, he claimed Monterey for the Spanish Crown. After his momentous discovery, attention to Monterey's port remained mysteriously obscured and lost in time. Alta California's long coast had attracted sea explorers under various foreign flags, and the viceroy in Mexico City, under the direction of the Spanish Crown, forged ahead with plans to establish Alta California's first mission colony and presidio. Father Serra was well known for his miraculous conversions of resistant indigenous natives reportedly of fierce behavior. He would march with the founding parties through Baja into San Diego, reaching the port that was discovered by Cabrillo over two centuries earlier. It was a period when missions were built of natural poles and made from simple walls of tule reeds or branches covered in mud, leaves, or straw and with sod roofs. Father Serra traveled the jungles of Mexico and the deserts of Baja by foot along the historic El Camino Real, overseeing his missions and ministering to a variety of native ethnicities, customs, and languages.

A Perfect Harbor

Spain's expedition to locate Monterey was led by Gasper de Portolá, the governor of Baja California. Portolá's first journey, which included Fr. Juan Crespí and a band of foot soldiers with 200 pack mules, began on July 14, 1769. The party located several known ports, including Santa Monica and Santa Barbara, and after walking the edge of the Pacific and reaching a precipice on the Big Sur coast, the men turned inland from the Santa Lucia Mountains. Eventually, Portolá reached the Salinas River camp called Blanco and sent scouts to find Monterey's harbor. They were unable to identify the features described already as the site for the new capital of Alta California, and they traveled as far north as Santa Cruz and the San Francisco Bay. Sighting a vast expanse of water, they still failed to identify Monterey or what was later called San Francisco's Golden Gate while mistaking each and concluding they had reached the brink of the ocean. Portolá gazed over the sweep of the northern coastline unaware that he was a few miles from Monterey's fabled harbor. On returning to San Diego on foot under driving winter snows, he was saved from lack of food only by curious friendly Indians. Portolá returned to the pioneer San Diego settlement to find near starvation conditions in the colony. The legendary explorer quickly calculated a supply route via overland trails to Baja and immediately planned a supply packet to arrive from Mexico's San Blas port. The galleon *San Antonio* had been delayed at first, finally arriving to restore the supplies needed by the desperate colonists wholly dependent on this support. After many delays, a small party began its second departure north to Monterey led by Portolá, returning along the same trail of discovery and reassured of success. On April 16, 1770, one day past Easter Sunday, the *San Antonio* finally departed from San Diego, with Fray Junípero Serra aboard and ready to join Portolá's overland party in Monterey.

The Early Settlement of Monterey

Monterey's presidio and mission were founded on June 3, 1770, after Gaspar de Portolá met the packet San Antonio and Father Serra stepped from a small boat onto the spot under an oak tree where Don Sebastián Vizcaíno claimed Monterey for Spain in 1602. A ceremony followed in the name of King Carlos III of Spain, and the second Spanish presidio and mission of Alta California was dedicated with the founding of Mission San Carlos Borromeo del Puerto de Monterey. Today, San Carlos Cathedral, or La Capilla Real, stands at the original mission site. By late 1771, permission had been granted from the Spanish Crown to move Mission San Carlos Borromeo to the river's edge in the verdant hills of Carmel Valley, relocating the mission away from the military presidio. Mission San Carlos Borromeo del Río Carmelo became permanent headquarters for all 21 of Alta California's historic missions. During his lifetime, Father Serra founded nine of the earliest missions. Carmel recorded its first baptism at the mission, which required all neophyte children to be immediately segregated from their families. Indigenous locals learned trade and building skills laboring to construct the missions. After Father Serra died in 1784, Father Lasuén began building a new stone chapel at the presidio. Spanish governor Felipe de Neves sent for stonecutter, mason, and craftsman Miguel Esteban Ruiz, who designed and built La Capilla Real at the presidio by 1795, and the Carmel mission was completed in 1797. In 1856, Mission San Carlos Borromeo del Río Carmelo again piqued public interest after it identified Father Serra's remains, discovered buried beneath the mission floor of the church with three of the first friars. The discovery of California's pioneers would be ceremoniously commemorated in 1884, and the mission's Fr. Angelo Casanova hosted 400 dignitaries to a ceremony officially identifying the tomb under the church and the remains of it founder, Fr. Junípero Serra.

Father Serra's Mission Chain

Mission San Carlos Borromeo del Río Carmelo would realize Father Serra's utopian dream as the permanent place to preside over his mission colonies. Each mission would be built within a single day's journey along El Camino Real. In 1771, after its humble beginning in Carmel, where the first church buildings of Mission San Carlos Borromeo de Río Carmelo were raised, Father Serra made a day's journey to Jolon, towards the encampment on the southern Camino Real near the prominent Santa Lucia Range, where Portolá previously camped with his exploratory party. Father Serra christened the river San Antonio, and near its banks, he raised bells in the high branches of a nearby live oak, tolling them in dedication of his third mission, Mission San Antonio de Padua, on July 14, 1771. In later years, mission president Fr. Fermín Lasuén founded the 13th mission, Mission Señora de la Soledad, on October 9, 1791; and the 15th, Mission San Juan Bautista, was dedicated on June 24, 1797. The great chain of missions prospered throughout the fertile regions of Alta California and gathered many neophytes as converts to the colonies. Father Serra returned to San Diego to meet with the beloved explorer Lt. Col. Juan Bautista de Anza, commander of Spain's frontier missions in the southwest. De Anza's men endured a rugged 1,210-mile desert journey: coming from Mexico on foot, they emerged from the Sonoran Desert at Nogales to cross the Mohave Desert to the San Carlos Pass, and into San Gabriel to meet with Father Serra in San Diego. They began on the trail to Monterey on April 18, 1774, leading a larger second expedition over land to settle the colony named for Saint Francis on October 9, 1776. This became California's third presidio and a new mission, Mission San Francisco de Asís. It was called Mission Dolores after a small creek there named by de Anza. It was the sixth California mission in a period of history serendipitously coinciding with the early years of the American Revolution. New settlers would come to Alta California along the de Anza trail bringing names of many famous citizens in Monterey's future, including Vallejos, Berryessas, Castros, and Bernals.

One

The Treasure of Monterey

Mission San Carlos Borroméo del Rio Carmelo

The Mission San Carlos Borromeo del Río Carmelo's elegant stone bell tower was built in 1797 and remains the only standing of the original California missions. Fr. Junípero Serra relocated this mission after leaving its first location at Monterey's presidio in 1771, segregating the military from the mission's native neophyte community. The mission became the home of all mission presidents in Alta California. (Anderson family collection.)

A commemorative wooden cross was raised near the spot (now on Recreation Trail) where explorer Gaspar de Portolá and Fr. Junípero Serra united their land and sea parties on the discovery of Monterey on June 3, 1770. The cross symbolizes the Spanish Crown's claim, and a press photograph from the 1960s commemorates this date. Portolá's first expedition from San Diego would suffer extreme hardship from the lack of supplies in 1769. During a snowstorm, he was unable to determine Monterey's location and departed after raising a first cross at the mouth of San Jose Creek near Pacific Grove and another atop a hill in the Carmel River's estuary. The expedition had been waiting for the supply ship *San José*, later reckoned lost at sea. Struggling to keep his party from starving, Portolá retreated back to the San Diego settlement. Portolá was in great doubt about supplies arriving for his explorations and dismayed about a second journey north to reach Monterey; Father Serra responded by initiating a novena mass praying for the colony's survival. On the ninth and last afternoon, the supply ship *San Antonio* was seen through the mist sailing directly towards San Diego's harbor. The following Sunday, Easter, would be joyously observed, and the day after, Father Serra departed San Diego aboard the *San Antonio* to found the new colony in Monterey. Father Serra met with Portolá's second land excursion, and a time of great levity with celebratory cannon fire further distanced indigenous people from the presence of the newcomers. (Author's collection.)

A native wood carved artifact rests within a small niche of the campanario. Mission Indians remained loyal to the Spanish padres through the long history of Mission San Carlos Borromeo del Río Carmelo from the earliest period of California settlement. (California History Room Archives, Monterey Public Library.)

Spanish sailor Vizcaíno, with three friars of the Carmelite order, discovered and named Río de Carmelo in January 1603 and conveyed to the Spanish Crown a spirited description of Monterey's harbor as an ideal future naval base. This location would be chosen by Father Serra in 1769, over 160 years after the first sighting. (California History Room Archives, Monterey Public Library.)

A photograph from a rare magic lantern transparency of 1906 reveals the mission's renovated shingle roof, added during the 1880s. This roof was effective at protecting the interior from further decay but was replaced in 1937 to match the pitch of the original. Note that the adjacent adobe ruins of the mission's quadrangle were worn into the ground by this time. The mission became an early landmark destination for visiting motorists. (Author's collection.)

A Mission San Carlos Borromeo del Río Carmelo centenarian native known as "Old Gabriel" took part in building the mission and was said to have lived to 151 years, often disputed nearer to 120 years. He had been baptized by Father Serra at the mission and died on March 14, 1890. (Southwest Museum of the American Indian Collection.)

In October, 1859, ownership of Mission San Carlos Borromeo del Río Carmelo was deeded back to the Catholic Church. By this time, roof tiles had been displaced, fallen, or stolen from the building, which had quickened the structure's deterioration. Although surrounded by many original adobe buildings, the mission was one of three in California to be built of cut stone. It was often visited during the 19th century, and families lined the stairs of the tower and mission entry nearing the century mark from its founding.

The most austere of all the mission chapels, the altar at Mission San Carlos Borromeo del Río Carmelo invokes a presence of the first Franciscan friars and founders of California. In 1856, Father Cayetano Sorertine had begun to explore beneath the ruins on the gospel side of the floor when he discovered a well-sealed vault. He observed "the body of a priest . . . luxuriously vested that none others had" and began a great renewed interest in the mission.

In 1926, during his restoration efforts at Monterey over 30 years, Father Ramón Mestres stands to the left of the cross marking the site of Serra's cell at the Mission San Carlos Borromeo del Rio Carmelo. To the right of the church is the priest's house designed by artist Jo J. Mora and museum dedicated to Harry Downie, restorer of the Monterey missions. (California History Room Archives, Monterey Public Library.)

Over 400 dignitaries gathered at Mission San Carlos Borromeo del Río Carmelo's ruins during the ceremonial opening of the burial vault under the church floor on July 3, 1882, overseen by Fr. Angelo Casanova. The remains entombed in the church floor were verified to be Friars Juan Crespí and Julian Lopes and mission presidents Fathers Fermín Lasuén and Junípero Serra. (California History Room Archives, Monterey Public Library.)

Mission San Carlos Borromeo del Rio Carmelo suffered great deterioration but remained standing for over a century. The massive stone church had been built by Serra's successor, Padre Fermín de Francisco Lasuén de Arasqueta, in 1793. Despite many hardships endured in earlier years, at the end of 1771, after settling the mission in Carmel, Father Serra's fantastic dream to expand the chain of missions continued with the founding of Mission San Antonio de Padua, 30 miles south.

The rededication of Mission San Carlos Borromeo del Rio Carmelo on August 28, 1884, occurred on the 100th anniversary of Father Serra's death. Father Casanova led a campaign to fund rebuilding that resulted in a new roof to protect the church's interior. (California History Room Archives, Monterey Public Library.)

The steps leading to the mission bells of the campanario at Mission San Carlos are accessible from the outer courtyard. All mission walls were finished with plastered stucco made from a mixture of water-slaked lime and sand as a finish to the exteriors. (California History Room Archives, Monterey Public Library.)

Father Serra lived the life of an ascetic in a hut adjacent to the early mission. A photograph of his cell and items used during his monastic duties as mission president are displayed, although he would never see the grand missions. Fr. Francisco Palou, his dearest friend and biographer from Baja, had succeeded him, and after a year, Father Lasuén took over the post of mission president. Each had resided at Mission San Carlos Borromeo del Rio Carmelo.

Nearly a century after its founding, Mission San Carlos Borromeo del Rio Carmelo stood as a relic of a forgotten era. In 1771, Father Serra's request during the first year in Monterey was granted, moving the mission to Carmel, a location that offered better soil, an adequate supply of fresh water along the river's edge, and proximity to a large Indian population, including local Costanoan, Salina, Rumsien, and Esselen natives.

Mission San Carlos Borromeo del Rio Carmelo is pictured around 1880. Before the repairs of 1884 to protect the building with a shingle roof, years of neglect were not an obstacle for local padres conducting services inside the chapel ruins. Church services continued under an open sky and kept alive the spirit of the first friars' dream. (California History Room Archives, Monterey Public Library.)

Mission San Carlos Borromeo del Rio Carmelo was the first of three mission churches built from stone; all others were made of adobe or burned brick. It was the only mission designed using an inverted catenary arch at the center of asymmetrical Moorish-styled towers.

The elegant star window allows morning sun to stream into the upper balcony, with added muted light from narrow windows at the church's sides. The building's eastern exposure has been studied at many missions and churches worldwide and proven as a feature creating brilliant illuminations within the church and altar on specific dates.

Complete restoration began in 1924 and continues today even as Mission San Carlos de Borromeo del Río Carmelo conducts important ceremonies. Many liturgical items were held in safekeeping at San Carlos Cathedral of Monterey after the mission was abandoned. Today, the Mission San Carlos de Borromeo del Río Carmelo holds many treasures to share from its earliest history. (Southwest Museum of the American Indian Collection.)

In 1936, the small chapel and shrine within the Mission San Carlos Borromeo del Río Carmelo's church near the southern courtyard were restored.

The first adobe home reportedly built in Monterey fell to ruin in 1898 and is preserved only through this image. It was constructed by and used as the residence of the first native neophyte baptized by Father Serra at Mission San Carlos Borromeo del Río Carmelo. (Southwest Museum of the American Indian Collection.)

The cornerstone of Mission San Carlos Borromeo del Río Carmelo was laid on July 7, 1793 and dedicated in September 1797 by Fr. Fermín Francisco de Lasuén. Father Serra made his last journey along El Camino Real to Carmel during his 70th year, and his death occurred there in 1784. He never would see the great Mission San Carlos Borromeo del Río Carmelo known today, but many surrounding communities shared the legacy of the famous friar's founding vision.

An early photograph depicts the open church ruins when serving occasional masses under the stars at Mission San Carlos Borromeo del Río Carmelo around 1856. With the church fallen in ruins, the discovery of the burial vaults of the first friars brought public attention to the old mission. (California History Room Archives, Monterey Public Library.)

The original 18th-century portrait of Fr. Junípero Serra, the ambitious founder of the missions of California, is lost in time, however, this sole photograph of it exists on a lantern slide. Although the Franciscan friars were well advanced in their daily writings, contemporary illustrations depicting their likenesses were few. (Southwest Museum of the American Indian Collection.)

Mission San Carlos Borromeo del Río Carmelo's church interior is pictured in 1936 in a view facing towards the altar as it appeared after 1924. Harry W. Downie, a master cabinet builder, began working on Mission San Carlos Borromeo del Río Carmelo and supervised the rebuilding of several missions in the Monterey area over 30 years.

This view depicts the church's interior entry prior to final restoration at the Mission San Carlos Borromeo del Río Carmelo. Note the baptistery door gate to the right as well as an intense flood of morning light into the balcony from the eastern-facing star window.

This image of Mission San Carlos Borromeo del Río Carmelo shows its first restored roof around 1884. The location is opposite the landmark hill (at upper left) on which Gasper de Portolá raised a cross in 1769. He had returned to Carmel from San Diego, founding Monterey with Father Serra in 1770. (California History Room Archives, Monterey Public Library.)

Renovations continued at the Mission San Carlos Borromeo del Río Carmelo, and it was rededicated as a parish church in 1933. Authentic architectural features had been designed under Harry W. Downie, a prominent authority on restoration who was aided by skilled craftsmen.

The loss of the church's roofing tiles over the years caused Mission San Carlos Borromeo del Río Carmelo to fall into complete disrepair until the advent of Fr. Angelo Delfino Casanova's 1882 restoration. His efforts created a new roof, but it would again need a corrected pitch and design to bring the old structure back to support clay tiles.

The Mission San Carlos Borromeo del Río Carmelo roof had been reframed in 1936, returning the design to an authentic profile. The New Deal brought Civilian Conservation Corps (CCC) builders and technicians to the venerable edifice. The original mission was first designed and built in 1797 by stonecutter and mason Manuel Esteban Ruiz. He was a native of Spain and had been commissioned a few years earlier to build San Carlos Cathedral in Monterey, completed in 1795.

On May 13, 1936, the CCC crew would near completion for framing the corrected pitch of the mission's roof for the addition of clay tiles. The southern grounds of the mission shown in this photograph continued to be developed as a courtyard and patio. The area gave access to the stairs of the mission campanario.

A scale model created during the restoration of Mission San Carlos de Borromeo del Río Carmelo had helped guide the restoration process. Harry Downie, master craftsman, sits with Msgr. Michael D. O'Connell, pastor of Carmel Mission, reviewing the necessary work it would take to accomplish the task. (California History Room Archives, Monterey Public Library.)

Squaring logs with a traditional adze, Harry Downie spent his career acquiring and mastering the skills required to use implements employed in authentic restorations in every detail. His approach fused modern ideas, materials, and tools to accomplish the goals and guided all the missions into recovery documented throughout this book. (California History Room Archives, Monterey Public Library)

Reconstruction of the adobe brick building at the mission's southeast side houses the Mora Chapel, dedicated to Father Serra. The mission roof framing was readied for traditional burned clay tiles. Original techniques were used to make adobe bricks from mixtures of mud, straw, and the natural stabilizer bitumen poured into molds, baked in the sun to harden, and set on end to finish the process. Each brick weighs about 60 pounds.

The 18th-century Spanish master mason and stonecutter Manual Esteban Ruiz arrived in Alta California followed by a line of several highly skilled builders and journeymen. He came at the time the third mission president, Father Lasuén, was planning the building of Mission San Carlos Borromeo del Río Carmelo. This grand edifice of cut stone would take several years to complete. Afterwards, Ruiz left California to retire in Mexico, leaving his masterworks behind to the ages.

A cornerstone ceremony commemorated the reconstruction of Mission San Carlos Borromeo del Río Carmelo on October 21, 1921. Manuel Onesimo, a descendant of Juan Onesimo, an Indian builder of the original mission who was baptized by Father Serra, and Manuel's son Alejandro bear the cornerstone blessed by Father Mestres. (California History Room Archives, Monterey Public Library.)

The cenotaph memorial adds visual beauty to the sacred burial site at the mission. Father Serra's sculpture was created by Jo J. Mora as a tribute to California's founder and was unveiled on October 12, 1924. Mora was a famed resident of Carmel who had lived among Indians in the Southwest and was well known for his creative Western art and his relationship to Native American history.

Pres. Dwight D. (right foreground) and Mamie Eisenhower are pictured visiting the famed Mission San Carlos Borromeo del Río Carmelo and Msgr. Michael O'Connell (left) on August 25, 1956. This was part of a well-known series of working tours made by the president with his wife. During this trip, he stayed at Pebble Beach's Cypress Point Golf Club. (California History Room Archives, Monterey Public Library.)

This photograph shows Cristiano Machado, a Mission San Carlos Borromeo del Río Carmelo caretaker and orchard master from 1877 to 1907. Of Portuguese Azorean descent, he was born in 1838 and was a former shore whaler. As a captain with the Carmel Whaling Company, Machado helped reestablish the orchard and participated in the mission restoration that led to the discovery of friars' burial sites, including Father Serra's. (California History Room Archives, Monterey Public Library.)

Mission San Carlos Borromeo del Río Carmelo's swallows appear nesting in the mission tower. To the bottom left is the revered life-sized *Our Lady of Bethlehem*, or *La Conquistadora*, a statue presented to the founders of the first Mission San Diego de Alcalá in 1769. That following year, Father Serra sailed into Monterey carrying the full-sized iconic statue to the Mission San Carlos Borromeo del Río Carmelo altar. In modern times, it was reunited with a vital missing piece when the Christ child was brought back to her arms from Mission San José. The statue resides in the mission after generations of caretaking by local families. It may be seen at the Mission San Carlos Borromeo del Río Carmelo in the mortuary chapel. (California History Room Archives, Monterey Public Library.)

Recreated from atop bared foundations, this adobe priest's quarters, a part of the restoration project during the 1930s, was designed by Jo J. Mora, artisan of the cenotaph memorial for Father Serra and other buildings at the mission. The reconstructed rectory stands in the forecourt of the mission and houses the Harry Downie Museum, with interpretive displays and artifacts devoted to the mission restoration story. (Author's collection.)

Mission San Carlos Borromeo del Río Carmelo is viewed from the west in its verdant setting as it appeared at the beginning of the 20th century. Although the roof was historically incorrect, it protected the interior from further deterioration and later was removed and replaced according to the original design and pitch.

The permeating history of Mission San Carlos Borromeo del Río Carmelo is a meaningful experience to any devotee attending the church chapel. The Catholic Church and the Franciscan Order believe in the universality of one creator and invite all to attend. (California History Room Archives, Monterey Public Library.)

A Mission San Carlos Borromeo del Río Carmelo stereograph made in 1912 by Stereo-Travel clearly depicts the profile of the redesigned shingled roof of 1884. The steps leading to the belfry are visible to the left side of its stone tower.

After 1852, the Mission San Carlos Borromeo del Río Carmelo would seem doomed to demise. Its deteriorated roof framing collapsed, and the tile roof fell in. Although many tiles were destroyed or stolen, church artifacts had been preserved at Monterey's San Carlos Cathedral for safekeeping. (California History Room Archives, Monterey Public Library.)

The baptistery, a small private niche to the left of the entry, was a beginning ceremony for neophytes within Mission San Carlos Borromeo del Río Carmelo's church. This first church tradition brought inclusion to native neophytes, who would sincerely embrace religious ceremony and doctrine. The bronze font holding holy water was brought from Spain by Father Sarría in 1823.

The baptistery's gateway door reveals a place of mystical sacrament within the small cove of the church. The tradition of the baptism ceremony begins the neophyte's life and blended native cultures with acceptance of the Franciscan friar's trust and faith.

The Onesimo family, descendants of the native Rumsien and Esselen Mission Indians, poses before Mission San Carlos Borromeo del Río Carmelo around 1921. Many groups adapted their ways of life to the missions, and the Esselen people virtually disappeared as a once independent and distinct people. (California History Room Archives, Monterey Public Library.)

The ornately sculpted travertine marble cenotaph memorial crafted by artist Jo J. Mora portrays Fr. Junípero Serra in an ornate bronze casting. It was unveiled on October 12, 1924, on the south side of the entrance of the church. A grizzly bear cub at his feet represents California. As "Father of the Missions," he was a great visionary and an indefatigable mission president who founded nine California missions. (California History Room Archives, Monterey Public Library.)

A vintage view of the Mission San Carlos Borromeo del Río Carmelo from around 1928 shows the garden courtyard and entry before restoration was completed. Exotic Spanish architectural roots influenced use of stone, adobe, brick, and clay tiles incorporated into modern California designs. The first missions in Monterey were built of walls of standing logs and spaces filled with twigs and plastered smooth with mud. A roof would be supported by a row of wooden beams, covered with layers of sticks, branches, and leaves and a thatched topping. (Author's collection.)

Carmel became Father Serra's headquarters until his passing on August 28, 1784. Assisted in learning the customs and languages of the local people by friendly Baja mission Indians who accompanied him, his steady determination settled Alta California with a simple message. Not unaware of the task at hand, Father Serra wrote in 1772 hinting of the difficulties that lay ahead, "those who come possess good humor, for they may become rich . . . with troubles, and if he do not draw the plow, how can there be a harvest?"

Oriana Weatherbee Day painted all 21 California missions between 1877 and 1884. Her *Mission San Carlos Del Río Carmelo* shows the mission during the years of Mexico's independence after laws passed governing the secularized use of all mission properties. It became a society of Californios, vaqueros of Mexican ancestry living together with the Native Americans.

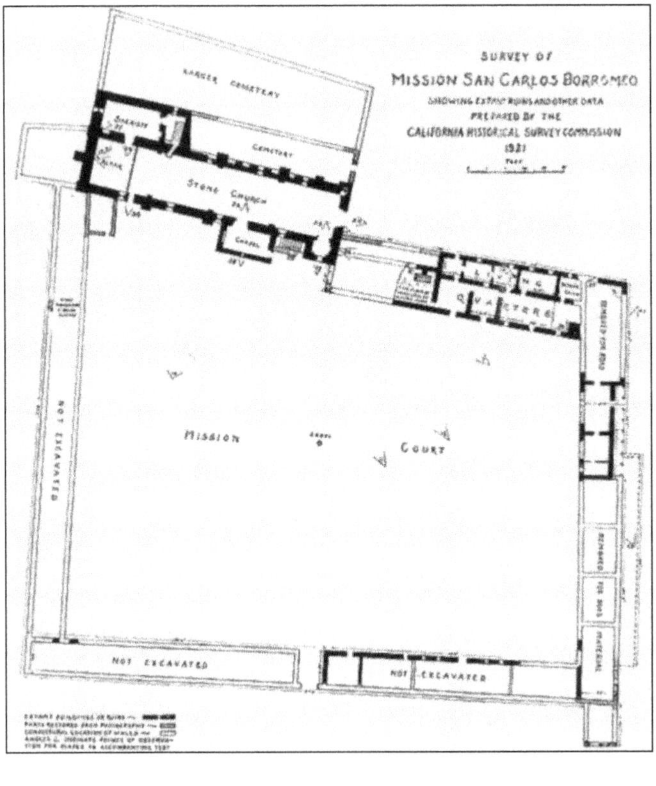

A measured drawing from the Historic American Building Survey depicts plans for the New Deal work program at Mission San Carlos Borromeo del Río Carmelo in 1933. Many familiar cities in California began as simple Franciscan missionary settlements supported by a diversified, thriving network of agricultural enterprise.

Two

Place of Perfect Peace
Mission San Antonio de Padua

After settling Mission San Carlos Borromeo del Río Carmelo in Carmel, Father Serra traveled with Fathers Miguel Pierras and Buenaventura Sitjar to the Santa Lucia Mountains to found the third mission of Alta California on July 14, 1771. In a setting along the original El Camino Real, Mission San Antonio de Padua was established next to a river named for St. Anthony in the valley in which Portolá had previously camped in 1769 that he called "La Hoya de la Sierra de Santa Lucia."

Cassiano, the oldest surviving member of his mission tribe at reportedly 132 years old, is pictured at Mission San Antonio de Padua. The first historic people of the area included Salinan, Esselen, and Yokuts tribes, who prospered with agriculture and diverse industries centered at the mission. The padres bred horses of excellent stock for which the mission became well known. (California History Room Archives, Monterey Public Library.)

Several rancherias run by neophytes in the Santa Lucia Mountains surrounded the mission property. The soil was well adapted to pasturelands, wheat, vineyards, and hardy crops. Fr. Buenaventura Sitjar, remaining at the mission for 27 years until 1808, developed an elaborate water system over 12 miles of aqueducts that diverted water throughout the mission property to serve its residents and industries. (Author's collection.)

Considered an omen at its founding, a lone native Indian witnessed the consecration of Mission San Antonio de Padua by Father Serra on July 14, 1771. Due to drought conditions, the first adobe mission was moved over a mile to its present site in 1810. Modern restorations begun in 1903 by the California Historical Landmarks League and Native Sons of the Golden West were continued after the rebuilt mission suffered damage caused by the 1906 San Andreas earthquake.

The church's walls crumbled into the foundations at Mission San Antonio de Padua before the beginning of the 20th century. It was lovingly restored by 1949 with funding from the Hearst Foundation. The 1810 church's condition, as with most early missions, required tearing it down to its footings. In 1805, nearly 1,900 neophytes worshiped at Mission San Antonio de Padua. The church at the mission remained one of the largest constructed throughout the entire chain until the 15th, Mission San Juan Bautista, was founded by Father Lasuén in 1797.

A group photograph shows local Indian descendants and generations of other residents on June 1, 1910, at Mission San Antonio de Padua's 89th anniversary. (California History Room Archives, Monterey Public Library.)

Mission San Antonio de Padua's church became a restoration project led by the California Historic Landmarks League. The chapel's final restoration was completed in 1949, guided by Harry Downie, the restorer of Mission San Carlos Borromeo del Río Carmelo in Carmel.

Designed with its distinctive burned-brick *fachada* that had remained standing over a century leading to the entry of its grand mission church, Mission San Antonio de Padua's solitary location made it one of the best preserved of all mission properties in California. This photograph, taken during the mid-1930s, shows the church entry with two solitary gravesites of former parishioners. (Author's collection.)

The mission interior was restored after 1949 to include the original wine cellar below ground level. The mission stored harvests and made sacramental wine with a wooden press that is now on display. This photograph, taken in 1934, reveals a remaining structure considered a wine vat adjacent to the mission vineyard. Mission Indians participated in the tending of farms and rich resources in the fertile San Antonio Valley.

An 1898 Photochrom of the Mission San Antonio de Padua reveals a diminishing luster after a prosperous lifetime. In a beautiful valley setting laden with live oaks on the banks of the San Antonio River, the third Alta California mission was consecrated by Fr. Serra in 1771 within six weeks of founding his second mission, Mission San Carlos de Borromeo del Rio Carmelo. Note the masthead busts left by passing English mariners, which are still seen displayed in front at the mission.

The Royal Road, or El Camino Real, passed through the San Antonio Valley and 35 miles on foot from Mission San Carlos de Borromeo in Carmel. The main trail north was moved to what is now the US Highway 101 location, and east about 20 miles towards King City. Left in solitude near a large military base, Fort Hunter Liggitt, and surrounded by farmsteads, Mission San Antonio de Padua was left relatively untouched and in better condition for restoration than all other missions in California. It was the first mission to produce quantities of burned brick for structural materials, as well as fired clay roof and aqueduct tiles. (Southwest Museum of the American Indian Collection.)

Pictured are corn grinding millstones and an old wooden wheel from a Spanish-style *caretta*, or oxen cart, at the mission. The San Antonio Valley was fed water that flowed from a high-elevation source to a stone-lined dam built by the early friars. Father Buenaventura Sitjar used San Miguel Creek; later, he courageously tapped into the San Antonio River and constructed a ditch more than three miles up the canyon. The flow of water through dams, open flumes, and masonry conduits fed the mission property and ran a water-driven wheel to stock its granary. Water allowed the missionaries to develop pastures, fields of grain, orchards, and vineyards. (Southwest Museum of the American Indian Collection.)

After the death of its last resident priest, Rev. Dorotéo Ambris, Mission San Antonio de Padua's structures slowly declined from long years of neglect. The increasing populations managed the rich grazing and agriculture resources, a tannery, a grain mill, workshops, orchards, and vineyards. This view of the mission is from the southwest around 1905.

In this 1910 photograph from the Historic American Building Survey records, the mission church has nearly been decimated, and monastery archways are visibly returning to the soil. Degradation of early California structures became a modern concern. Mission San Antonio de Padua was considered the best preserved of all mission properties because of its location away from civilization.

By 1828, the mission had 20,118 animals, including 8,000 cattle and 10,000 sheep. In 1833, decreasing populations under the Mexican government's secularization of the missions led to the appearance of Zacatecan Franciscans from Mexico who oversaw the dwindling population of less than 300 as well as the mission's industries.

Mission San Antonio de Padua's profile in a 1934 survey photograph reveals the standing *espadaña* bell tower within its unique burned-brick facade. The venerable old olive tree planted in 1834 stands even grander today.

In the 1920s at Mission San Antonio de Padua, few repairs were made to the burned-brick walls. The mission property, surrounded today by a large military preserve, was left pristine, with untouched archives for restorers and archaeologists. (Anderson family collection.)

A turn-of-the-century image shows the mission altar used for services on completion of the first modern restoration by the California Historical Landmarks League in 1907. Harry Downie, a famed restorer from Carmel, added Mission San Antonio de Padua to his projects in 1948 to bring it back to the wonderfully restored condition visitors experience today. (Southwest Museum of the American Indian Collection.)

A Photochrom from 1898 depicts the mission's romantic setting and the distant Santa Lucia Mountains and surrounding valley. The mission became an early productive colony in the network of missions and created leather tanning, wax, candle, and soap industries along with a wide variety of agricultural products.

Exposed for a century to southeastern weathering, the 1810 brick *espadaña* has withstood the test of time in this c. 1934 photograph. During his residence, Fr. Buenaventura Sitjar, with his companion friars, developed surpluses that were sold that would provide clothing for the neophyte workers. At his passing in 1808, the mission was greatly productive, with over 3,000 converts baptized.

In a photograph from the 1850s, the mission appears isolated and neglected. Its last resident was a secular Mexican Indian priest, Rev. Dorotéo Ambris, who tended the mission from 1843 until his death in 1882. Soon after his passing, the structure was left to ruins.

Graceful archways remained of the portico completed in 1813. Master builders trained native neophyte labor under the guidance of the mission friars. Columns of the mission's unique facade were constructed entirely of burned brick. Its walls were made of adobe bricks weighing nearly 60 pounds apiece. The mission fabricated clay roof tiles and exterior tiles.

Today, the arcade made of burned brick has been restored along with the original monastery with beautifully landscaped gardens displaying artifacts that include ancient millstones, a waterwheel, and ship's mastheads. The area's regional natural resources and agricultural assets were maintained by native Indian labor from established surrounding ranchos.

San Antonio de Padua has been an ideal destination for photographers to capture the out-of-the-way beauty of the mission's exquisite architecture and scenery. All visitors might experience the scene as a portal going back to the first friars and Alta California's founding.

By 1890, the archway cloister and the roofing had disappeared due to extreme weathering at Mission San Antonio de Padua. The property was abandoned by 1882 and left to curiosity seekers to observe efforts of reconstruction that eventually lasted into the mid-20th century.

An early statue of San Antonio de Padua held at Mission Santa Barbara's archives depicts the saint who was born in Portugal at the end of the 12th century. A Franciscan living in Italy and France, he left a stunning legacy of preaching with associated miracles. He was canonized as a saint within a year of his death in 1231. (Southwest Museum of the American Indian Collection.)

Curious natives were friendly with Father Serra at Mission San Antonio de Padua and offered gifts of pine nuts and seeds. Within two years' time, an adobe church was completed with dwellings for 150 settlers and converts. A short-lived rebellion came during 1775 as local natives wounded an Indian neophyte during baptism, causing soldiers to be sent from Monterey.

The original Mission San Antonio de Padua structures, built of adobe and clay tile roofing, were ready before 1800. During a severe drought, a second location was established just one mile away, and a much larger church was constructed with tall arched doorways and flanking buttress-like turrets topping its facade, which was considered graceful and elaborate. The cloistered archways, storerooms, barracks, warehouses, and shops were completed along with an excellent irrigation system for the fields and orchards. The new church had been finished in 1813 and was largely the work of neophyte masons.

The millpond was developed by the first friars to power the grain mill after draining into a penstock that drove a waterwheel. A covered area and stone threshing deck for winnowing were near where water ran the millstones to grind wheat the mission grew.

In 1913, the millpond and dam were restored by a local rancher to supply his water. This c. 1934 photograph shows the remaining structure after grain mill and waterwheel had stopped operating decades before.

The vaulted roof and chamber above the waterwheel allowed gravity-fed water to turn it with pressure, turning its horizontal wheel in the chamber below. It was one of many innovations created by the early friars at the mission.

In 1778, a stone-lined dam and earthen ditch would supply water to the center of the mission area. The millpond spillway powered grist stones by 1806. Water traveled past the tannery to the waterwheel and then flooded the fields and orchards below.

Mission San Antonio de Padua lost most of it church walls, but the burned-brick facade remained. Because of its remote location, the property today has remained a trove of discovery for archaeologists studying Alta California's pioneer days.

Mission San Antonio de Padua became greatly affected by the famous 1906 earthquake along the San Andreas Fault, which followed the first restoration. Because of the mission's early role in the establishment of Alta California settlements, the restoration project was attended by several organizations and funding sources, including the Hearst Foundation between 1948 and 1949.

An adobe orchardist's home existed in harmony with the mission property, which was largely run by neophyte Indians. Mission San Antonio de Padua became a successful colony because of this agreeable relationship with indigenous people, and it grew to a converted population of over 2,000.

The ruins of Mission San Antonio de Padua's arched portico and church in 1890 show longtime neglect. Father Gutiérrez counted 4,651 baptisms at the mission in 1844.

By the late 1890s, new activities around the mission grounds had begun, and large beams and planks were stacked for repairs of the church. The efforts were continued in 1903 by Joseph R. Knowland of Oakland with the California Historical Landmarks League, but the project was slowed down after the 1906 earthquake, when the vaulted dome of the church was partially destroyed. The unique architecture was created by forming a huge mound of earth that was later removed. The church footings measured 40 feet by 200 feet.

Once, the authentic El Camino Real roamed through the San Antonio Valley by Mission San Antonio de Padua, but the mission soon became a distant part of the landscape. Being surrounded by Fort Hunter Liggett and private acreage helped keep its structural appearance untouched, and the immense thickness of its adobe walls resisted wear.

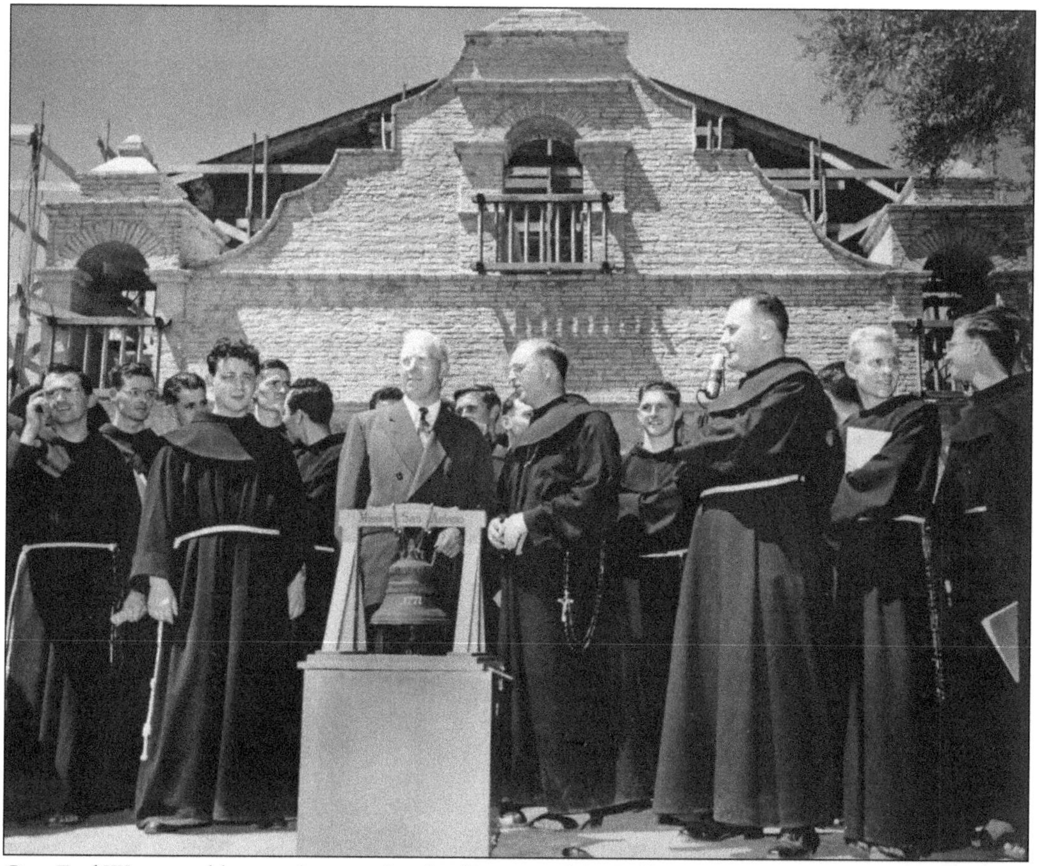

Gov. Earl Warren addresses the crowd at the "Return of the Bells" ceremony at Mission San Antonio de Padua in 1949. Members of the Franciscan Order returned one of the mission's original bells, which had been held for safekeeping at Mission San Carlos Borromeo. It is now centered within the mission *espadaña*. (California History Room Archives, Monterey Public Library.)

As it has for centuries, Mission San Antonio de Padua lies near an undistributed rural plateau of oak trees on the bank of San Miguel Creek. By 1934, the church stood with a wooden roof over it, while the monastery was not yet rebuilt.

Mission San Antonio de Padua, a painting by Oriana Weatherbee Day, portrays the mission after 1877, showing the days after the introduction of the secularization laws. Rev. Dorotéo Ambris, the last resident priest, would care for the property until his death in 1882.

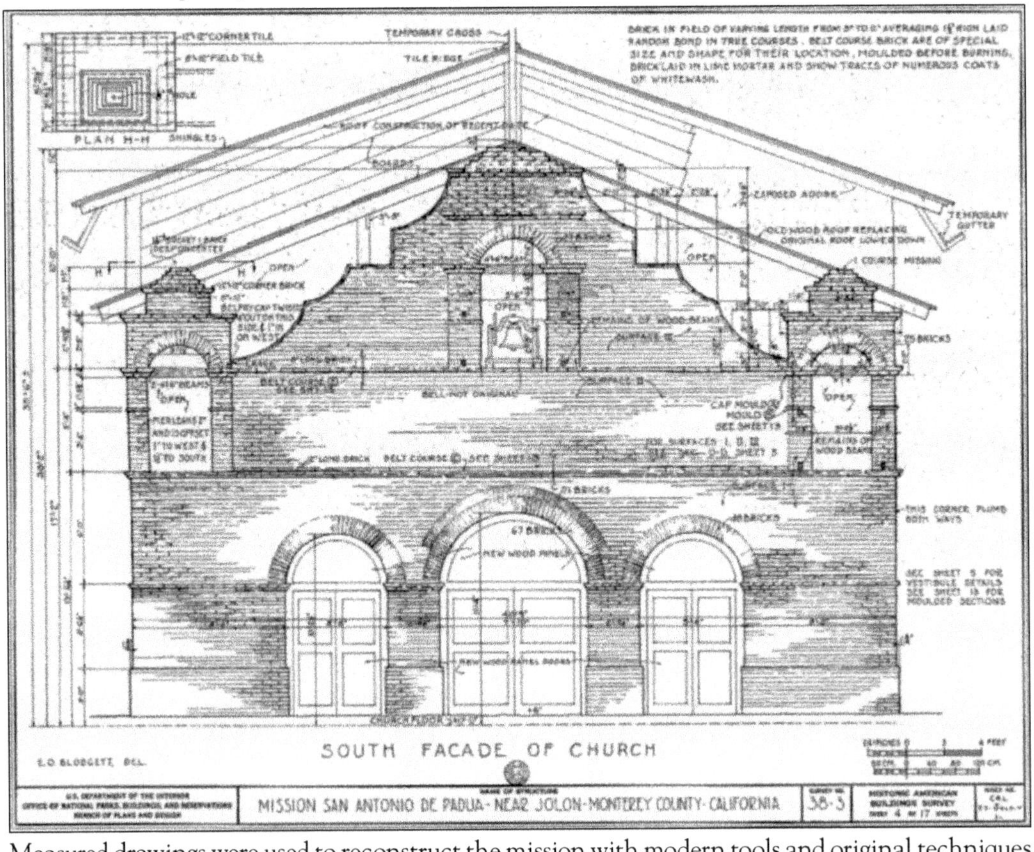

Measured drawings were used to reconstruct the mission with modern tools and original techniques to complete the process. Mission San Antonio de Padua stands today as a living monument to California's history and the founding friars.

Three

Solace of Soledad

Mission Nuestra Señora de la Soledad

Nuestra Señora de la Soledad was named by explorer Gaspar de Portolá after hearing a native murmur similar syllables. The site was discovered during his expeditions overland to discover Monterey. The Mission Nuestra Señora de la Soledad was founded on October 9, 1791, by Fr. Fermín Lasuén and erected on the bleak western plain of the Salinas River. Here, curious Sunday-attired onlookers in 1902 explore its ruins. This recurring complication of the mission's history would hinder many opportunities for careful archeology in later years.

A rare 1906 magic lantern photograph reveals the mission's waning profile in ruins. Mission Nuestra Señora de la Soledad became a popular out-of-the-way attraction and a subject continuously photographed through the years in various states of ruin. (Author's collection.)

By 1938, the adobe ruins of Mission Nuestra Señora de la Soledad were excavated. The mission was rebuilt by Harry Downie in 1955. He was the craftsman who guided reconstruction of all the Monterey missions discussed within this volume. The adobe convento wing shown in this photograph would be renovated in 1962.

A dramatic postcard view depicts the symbolic cross framed within the Mission Nuestra Señora de la Soledad ruins. Soledad, the 13th mission, was founded only weeks after Father Lasuén's dedication of Mission la Exaltacion de la Santa Cruz. It was considered a halfway stop along El Camino Real between Missions Santa Clara de Asís and San Antonio de Padua. Nearly 200 natives gathered at mission grounds in less than two years, by the end of 1796.

A place of solace, Mission Nuestra Señora de la Soledad was a haven for many seeking cooler shade from the dry, excessive heat of this area's summer weather. The landscape was less abundant for farming and was prone to floods from the nearby Salinas River.

An early view shows life as it existed at the church and attached convento building to the right. Mission Nuestra Señora de la Soledad remained vulnerable to rapid deterioration over the years, being located within an arid climate and prone to flash flooding from heavy rains. As adobe buildings to the rear were returning into earthen hills, the mission would begin to vanish.

Mission Nuestra Señora de la Soledad's church and convento ruins are pictured around 1928. In central California, old Mission Nuestra Señora de la Soledad became an escape for fleeing Monterey citizens at the time of the French pirate Hippolyte de Bouchard's 1818 invasion with 360 men under the Argentine flag. Bouchard attacked Monterey's harbor and vandalized its abandoned buildings for a week. (Author's collection.)

By 1811, nearly 600 neophytes were part of the mission and dedicated their work to leading quiet, peaceful lives. After Mission Nuestra Señora de la Soledad's decline, its last missionary, Father Sarría, survived a few years past a secularization decree in 1834 united the mission property with neighboring Mission San Antonio de Padua and effectively ending Mission Nuestra Señora de la Soledad's days.

Our Lady of Sorrows is displayed in an altar niche and the namesake of Mission Nuestra Señora de la Soledad. It became the 13th mission established in California chain and ended services with its last resident Franciscan padre, Fr. Vicente Francisco Sarría. Upon his death in 1835, his body was carried on foot by neophyte Indians 35 miles to the Mission San Antonio de Padua for burial, and soon after, Mission Nuestra Señora de la Soledad was abandoned.

The Mission Nuestra Señora de la Soledad is a perfect place of peace, as it was during the days of Portolá's arrival. It was restored to its former beauty in 1955, and its location in a remote part of Monterey County is just a few miles from today's El Camino Real. (Author's collection.)

In the 1950s, mission grounds were bladed with a bulldozer to below ground level, removing all debris and allowing the mission to be reconstructed from scratch. Any chances for archaeology were lost after this—except in the untouched soils nearby.

Harry Downie, the famed restorer of the Mission San Carlos Borromeo del Río Carmelo, cleared the ruins to begin a careful re-creation of the mission structures by 1955. The adjacent convento was completed in 1963.

Mission Nuestra Señora de la Soledad's thick adobe walls remained untouched and neglected for decades after its abandonment. As was the destiny for most mission buildings, the restoration process came to the ruins to preserve as authentically as possible California's history.

The natural isolation of Mission Nuestra Señora de la Soledad, west of today's El Camino Real, is seen in this c. 1918 photograph of the ruins, a bleak silhouette against the sky. Only Mission Santa Barbara and San Carlos Cathedral in Monterey had continued occupations past the 1830s under the original Franciscan padres.

By 1841, an inspection of assets during Mexican secularization reported a noticeable decline in the vineyards, orchards, and gardens, which had all gone wild. Many surrounding ranchos continued pastureland farming through the next decades.

Adobe walls of Mission Nuestra Señora de la Soledad around 1902 show age and weathering from the moisture of cold, harsh winters. Adobe was especially susceptible to degradation without proper roofing and often would cave in.

A c. 1939 view of Mission Nuestra Señora de la Soledad shows the church to the left of the mission convento. Only a mile west of the Salinas River, the property is surrounded by thousands of barren acres mostly consigned to pastures. Throughout the mission years, it was subjected to frequent flooding during California's rainy seasons.

Sculpted ruins of Mission Nuestra Señora de la Soledad are pictured in stunning detail around 1932. The first mission church was completed in 1797, then rebuilt in 1803. Situated on the Salinas plains, it was tended by Fr. Florencio Ibanez for over 15 years. He ministered the last days of his friend Don José Joaquín de Arrillaga, the governor of Alta California who died at the mission in 1814 and was buried beneath the church floor. The last missionary there, Fr. Vincente Francisco Sarría, refused to forsake his small flock and leave at the time of Mexico's ownership. He remained, in destitution and enfeebled by age, dying at the altar. (Author's collection.)

The Mission Nuestra Señora de la Soledad accounted for 289 neophytes in a 1796 report, only half that of Mission la Exaltacion de la Santa Cruz. The above photograph of the mission's condition around 1882 shows the area as a feedlot surrounding the ruins. Below, a productive pasture frames the ruins in the foreground around 1936.

Mission Nuestra Señora de la Soledad is pictured in the 1930s surrounded by a working cattle farm as in the days of the Californios of Alta California. Newly discovered photographs reveal a forlorn open landscape that was at times arid but often chilled by fog, making life in adobe living quarters difficult to endure. (Both, Anderson family collection.)

Lined up like oversized pins positioned to topple, the remaining adobe foundations of the Mission Nuestra Señora de la Soledad from 1808 were close to disappearing forever. In 1954, Harry Downie, master restorer of the Carmel Mission, would begin to rebuild the structure from the ground up, first leveling the remaining ruins. He continued rebuilding the adjacent convento, overseeing its completion in 1962. (Author's collection.)

In a c. 1898 photograph, massive three-foot-thick walls support structural hand-hewn timbers to anchor the walls and roof of the building. The walls of adobe brick were resistant despite years of pounding rainstorms.

This c. 1858 photograph at Mission Nuestra Señora de la Soledad is a perfect family portrait. Hay and feed were sold near the ruins, and grazing had been the main resource of the surrounding community. Living conditions were a challenge, and the mission clergy changed frequently.

The first temporary adobe structure was erected in 1797 at Mission Nuestra Señora de la Soledad, and a new church was built in 1808. The convento wing had begun to disappear by the time this 1850s photograph was made.

The collapsed structure of Mission Nuestra Señora de la Soledad in 1905 was dramatically situated in the center of vast acreage. Loss of the mission's roofing caused significant decay, as the rafters had caved into the adobe walls.

The timbers for roof support had been hand hewn from pines from the Santa Lucia foothills. Abundant natural resources helped support all of the mission properties as they became prosperous colonies.

Due to its remote location and lack of fertile soil, the mission was not productive, and it was abandoned after 1835. The location of the mission was greatly affected by the Salinas River flooding the land and buildings several times during the 19th century.

Pictured near the turn of the century, Mission Nuestra Señora de la Soledad was long neglected and had a short life span as an active mission. Over 30 padres took the lonely post at the mission, and Fr. Ibanez, broken and crippled from age, stayed the longest because there was no replacement for him. (Southwest Museum of the American Indian Collection.)

The site at Mission Nuestra Señora de la Soledad was a part of California's earliest history. In 1769, it was along the path to establish Monterey's harbor, presidio, and mission. The ruins of Mission Nuestra Señora de la Soledad have become revered by those on an adventurous path to exploring places—not unlike the Egyptian pyramids or other world wonders.

Life at Mission Nuestra Señora de la Soledad during the early 19th century was centered on farming—until 1835, when the mission had become an abandoned outpost, as depicted in the painting *Mission Nuestra Señora de la Soledad* by Oriana Weatherbee Day. The artist portrayed surrounding daily life and completed 19th-century renderings of all of California's missions during her lifetime.

Four

SAN CARLOS CATHEDRAL
LA CAPILLA REAL

The title San Carlos Cathedral had been given to La Capilla Real, or the Royal Chapel, in 1967. This is Monterey's oldest surviving building, in continuous use since 1795. The chapel was built upon the site of Mission San Carlos Borromeo del Puerto de Monterey after its relocation to Carmel and was founded by Father Serra in 1770 at Monterey's first presidio. San Carlos Cathedral was historically the key church for the political life of the province. (Author's collection.)

The first mission chapel and presidio of Monterey were founded on the same day by Fr. Junípero Serra and the governor of Baja, Gaspar de Portolá, upon uniting sea and land parties at the famous Vizcaíno-Serra Oak at the harbor on June 3, 1770. San Carlos Cathedral was the first cathedral and first cut-stone, architect-designed building in California.

Fr. Ramón Mestres poses by the aged Vizcaíno-Serra Oak, the legendary tree that spanned Monterey's history from the first discovery in 1602 to the founding of the mission and presidio in 1770. It was the meeting place of Father Serra and Governor Portolá. Replanting the tree was attempted 135 years later, after it was discovered floating in Monterey Bay following a storm. A dedication plaque that appears in this photograph had been added in 1905. Today, the oak is no longer standing, but a small piece can be viewed at the San Carlos Cathedral museum. (Southwest Museum of the American Indian Collection.)

San Carlos Cathedral was built in the place of the original Mission San Carlos Borromeo del Puerto de Monterey after 1774. A new location of the mission allowed separation from the neophyte natives and presidio soldiers. The new Mission San Carlos Borromeo del Río Carmelo, established within the lush valley of the Carmel River, had become a successful agricultural settlement and permanent home for the mission president, Fr. Junípero Serra.

The elegant San Carlos Cathedral is captured in this c. 1928 photograph showing the entrance to the chapel lined with hedges and the iron entry gate. The design is considered the most graceful among California's mission architecture, with the chapel's elegant scrolled facade and Doric pilasters framing the unique centerpiece relief carving of *Our Lady of Guadalupe*, the only statue of its kind added to the missions.

The 19th-century confessional, place of contrition for the faithful, is among several fixtures and original artifacts within the chapel's interior. (Author's Collection)

The chapel's remodeling to a cruciform design was completed in 1858 to include transepts laterally extending the church nave. In 1942, the windows had been returned to original rectangular shapes to reflect the historical character and design with many other refinements made by Harry Downie, supervising restorer.

The iconic statuary and artwork of revered saints were used for reflection. *Nuestra Señora de Guadalupe*, *Christ*, and *St. Joseph* are displayed within the chapel's east altar in 1934.

This image shows the presidio of Monterey and San Carlos Cathedral during the mid-1930s and how the town had grown around it. The stone chapel was built in the center of the original presidio's walled fort, near today's shoreline in Lake Estero Park. Immediately after the Spanish landed, construction of the presidio began under the supervision of Miguel Costanso, an engineer who came with Father Serra aboard the *San Antonio*. At different times, settlers flew the flags of three countries—Spain (before 1822), Mexico (from 1822 to 1846), and the United States (from 1846 forward). In 1846, US Navy Pacific Squadron commodore John Drake Sloat signaled the passing of Mexican rule to the United States in a proclamation following the landing of 250 Marines and seamen on the shore on July 7. His act of raising the American flag at the Monterey Customhouse was backed with mutual acts of allegiance in San Francisco, Sonoma, and Sutter's Fort, Sacramento.

A silver liturgical object held at the San Carlos Cathedral is one of many treasures brought to Monterey by the founding friars. Father Serra's silver altar, brought with him by ship to Monterey, was portable and unfolded. (Southwest Museum of the American Indian Collection.)

Early Spanish liturgical items were stored for centuries at the San Carlos Cathedral for safekeeping during the decline of most California mission buildings. Hanging are censers used in High Mass and for special occasions requiring incense. Ceremonies would often present the items in sensuous chapel surroundings with clergy in vestments, elevating church attendees to a closer relationship to their faith. (Southwest Museum of the American Indian Collection.)

The San Carlos Cathedral entrance is shown with the ornately carved stone relief parapet and architecture. Barely visible below is a path leading to the entry of the chapel made from round whalebone tiles cemented with stone; it was later removed because of its uneven wear. (Author's Collection)

San Carlos Cathedral's west transept door leads into the church nave. The transoms carved of Carmel sandstone built over both doors were designed so visitors could enter the church from the midsection on opposing sides. The transepts were added to the building in 1858, expanding the chapel.

This image depicts the west transept door leading into the chapel, a perspective of the chapel's wall showing arched windows, installed in 1858 and later replaced by master restorer Harry Downie to their original openings and shape.

Monterey was the first of Alta California's northern settlements, and San Carlos Cathedral is the finest preserved building from the era. Often considered the most graceful and intricately carved of the mission churches, its stone features and its iconic tower have graced the Monterey area

San Carlos Cathedral was restored by Father Casanova, who in 1893 changed the bell tower from the original *espadaña* design and row of windows into a square tower that featured a tiled pyramidal rooftop. The building had been constructed of cut stone by master mason Manuel Ruiz of Spain from 1791 to 1795.

for over 200 years. This panoramic view shows a celebratory gathering at San Carlos Cathedral around 1910; at the left is the Young Men's Institute Hall, and at right is the rectory. (California History Room Archives, Monterey Public Library.)

The belfry is made from uneven rocks fit together to hold the supporting mechanisms for the bells. The tower windows were sculpted, arched openings that were redesigned during the 1890s.

Viewed from the northeast, the chapel's stucco exterior was applied over the stone in a traditional finish. The facade's center arch entrance is framed by a pilaster front and a parapet set forward of its gable roof. It is one of the oldest and most elaborate of all mission churches.

Part of the narrow passage to the bell tower's highest level reveals old steps worn from use over the ages. The chapel has been upgraded with seismic retrofitting to ensure occupants' safety.

In 1771, Father Serra had moved Monterey's first Mission San Carlos Borromeo del Puerto de Monterey to the present site by the Carmel River. Monterey became the capital of both Baja and Alta California in 1777. The Royal Chapel had been completed in 1775, then burned down, and the present stone building was rededicated in 1795.

The ancient steps that led to the belfry wind through dark passages opening to the bell enclosure. Walls of quarried sandstone were brought to the site for the mason and artisans under the direction of Manuel Ruiz, a Spanish stonecutter. He was the designer and builder of the Royal Chapel and also the Mission San Carlos Borromeo del Río Carmelo in following years.

The entrance to San Carlos Cathedral has changed over the years, bringing it to safe standards after the completion of renovations to all buildings; it was rededicated in 2009. The museum holds several rare objects from California's earliest founders, and at the site local archeologists continue to unearth the original remaining stone walls surrounding the first fort.

The fort at the presidio had been created during the time of the first settlement in Monterey in 1770 and was built of crude materials along with a few huts. Late in the 18th century, Spain erected a fort called El Castillo on the hill overlooking Monterey Bay, where the present presidio grounds are located; today, it is the site of the US Army Presidio of Monterey.

Fr. Angelo Casanova, Franciscan pastor from 1870 to 1893, installed a unique pathway of whalebone to enter the church interior. This was later removed during renovations to accommodate increasing public use.

The transept or lateral section added to the church in 1858 allowed more room and conformed to a traditional style of church architecture and also enlarged the original nave.

For centuries, San Carlos Cathedral, the church of all the Spanish and Mexican governors of Alta California, remained ministered by Franciscans who have safeguarded the early liturgical artifacts from California's founding. A wonderful history museum offers tours and displays the story of Monterey and many treasures of the past.

A vintage postcard of the chapel shows it as it appeared before its many modernizations. Unlike most of the Spanish missions, San Carlos Cathedral has not undergone severe, deteriorating ruin. (Author's Collection)

A statue of Fr. Junípero Serra was dedicated in 1891 overlooking the spot where he stepped onto Monterey's shore. The Spanish galleon *San Antonio* had anchored, and Gaspar de Portolá joined Father Serra by the oak tree commonly referred to as the Vizcaíno-Serra Oak. After completion of El Camino Real's trail to Monterey, the founding of Mission San Carlos Borromeo del Puerto de Monterey at the presidio was marked with a large celebration on June 3, 1770. The statue is located at the second Monterey presidio, El Castillo.

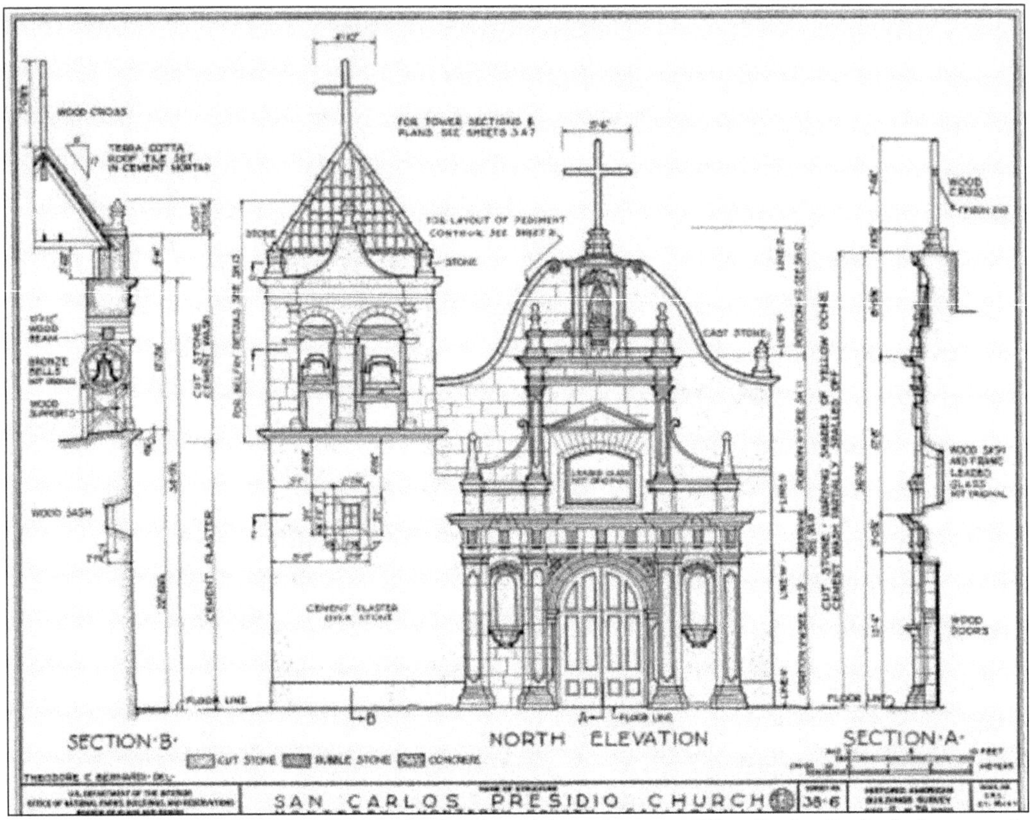

A measured elevation drawing showing both side and front features of San Carlos Cathedral was made by the Historic American Building Survey and used for 1933 New Deal restoration programs.

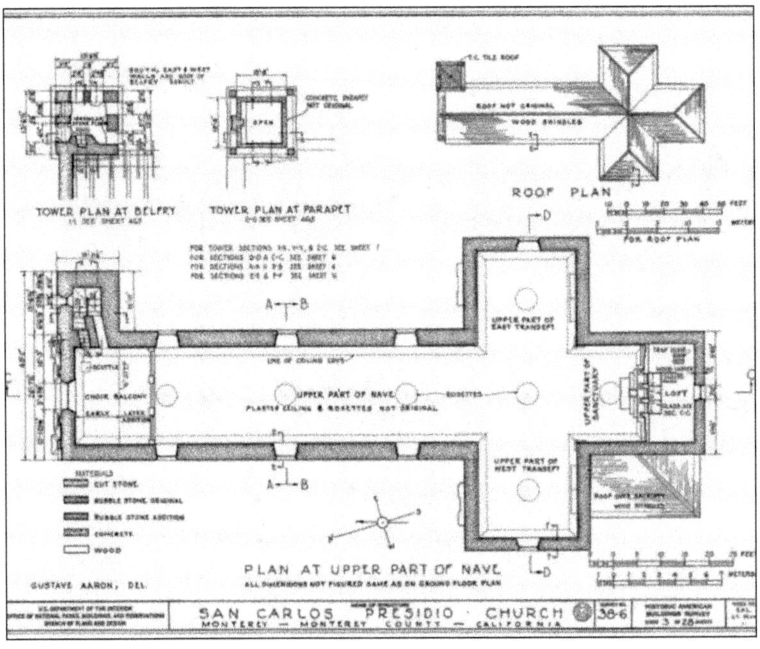

A floor plan used for San Carlos Cathedral depicts the church's cruciform design and tower base. Drawings used to restore mission buildings were created by architectural firms during the New Deal.

Five

Eastern Exposure
Mission San Juan Bautista

During the golden age of mission settlements, Father Lasuén's succession as mission president encouraged the founding of several missions to fulfill the tradition of spacing each within a day's travel. Mission San Juan Bautista was founded just 13 days after Mission San José, on June 27, 1797, and was the 15th mission. It was located in the center of a rich agricultural valley near a Mutsun Indian community. (Author's collection.)

Mission San Juan Bautista displayed a wooden tower from the 1860s that was later replaced. The mission attracted as many as 500 neophytes to its grounds by 1803, and new plans had been made to enlarge the church following an earthquake. Early Spanish occupation brought artisans and builders to work and train the neophytes. A Mutsun native village with homes built of willow and coarse grass stood on the eastern edge of the San Benito River valley and became part of the mission culture. The last full-blooded Mutsun Indian died in January 1930, and she is buried in the Indian cemetery beside the old mission church. (Anderson family collection.)

A postcard view of Mission San Juan Bautista after 1950 shows the masonry tower removed. There was interest at this time to use the mission for filming the movie *Vertigo*, the 1957 Alfred Hitchcock thriller. A stage set imitating stairs to the tower would be built in a nearby field to create the final takes.

The massive building rises elegantly above its buttressed walls and reaches over 40 feet in height. Leocadio Martinez completed construction of the mission church by 1812, and Mission San Juan Bautista's grand walls would measure 188 feet long by 72 feet wide.

By 1835, assets of the church were liquidated and the property divided among a population of 50 settlers of what became known as San Juan de Castro. Jose Tiburcio Castro became the secular administrator of the mission and auctioned off the properties under the new rules of Mexican secularization.

The west entry to Mission San Juan Bautista is shown around 1928. The arcade faces the town square on the original El Camino Real trail. The authentic Spanish town square, now part of the California State Parks system, surrounds the mission, which was subject to damage from multiple earthquakes in 1800, 1812, and 1906. The mission has been lovingly restored today to its full beauty. (Author's collection.)

A Spanish padre named Fr. Felipe del Arroyo de la Cuesta came to the mission in 1808 and walled in the interior spaces, separating it into three naves to create smaller, separate rooms after mission Indian populations decreased. The view from this postcard reveals the archways fully restored to their original design by the mid-1970s.

The entry at the Mission San Juan Bautista and monastery are shown in this c. 1934 photograph with the masonry bell tower, built in 1926, that replicated the old wooden one. By 1950, it too had been torn down as incompatible with the original mission's design.

The church sanctuary and altar of Mission San Juan Bautista was photographed in 1934. The church was briefly passed in 1833 to Zacatecan Franciscans, Mexican clergy who resided at the church during the advent of secularization laws.

A recently discovered c. 1928 photograph clearly shows details of the wooden scaffolding and bell in the garden near the church. Nine original bells were tolled from Mission San Juan Bautista's trees by the earliest friars, and a melodious music of the spheres rose up from the mission grounds. The bells had been cast in Peru and traditionally were used in trees or made to ring from a scaffold, a practice from the early days of Father Serra's first missions. A single original bell remained at Mission San Juan Bautista over many years as the others were scattered. Resident friars would toll the church bell from the garden patio to keep tradition for early-morning masses and evening vespers. The bell remains aloft at the northeast end of the church in a new *espadaña* replica tower near the entry to the church and gardens featuring a life-sized statue of Father Serra. (Author's collection.)

Taken from the rear of the church around 1928, this photograph shows the masonry campanario that was built to imitate the old wooden tower. It was later replaced with the present-day *espadaña* with three bells. (Author's collection.)

A rediscovered photograph of Mission San Juan Bautista's entry from the late 1920s shows an entry road into the square with a tiled canopy that was later removed. The mission structure had always remained intact and occupied by clergy throughout its long existence. (Author's collection.)

Among the iconic artifacts remaining at Mission San Juan Bautista, Our Lady of San Juan, dressed by natives within its altar niche, is displayed in unique white garb. The figure has stood over the centuries and would be sung to each evening with traditional themes such as "El Alabado," which means "The Praised."

The portico of the monastery faces homes, commercial buildings, and a livery as part of the original Spanish square. Mission San Juan Bautista's 230-foot-long arcade is perhaps the most photographed of all mission porticos. The large church features three aisles separated by archways and with separate altars.

The New England–style tower created in the 1860s rose above the San Benito River Valley for more than 60 years. Mission San Juan Bautista had grown to over 1,200 neophyte Indians, and more than 4,300 natives are buried in the old cemetery beside the northeast wall of the mission church next to Spanish Californians. (Author's collection.)

The lush gardens of Mission San Juan Bautista are pictured in 1934 with the earlier masonry bell tower and center fountain. As early as 1772, on St. Benedict's Day, Father Juan Crespi and Governor Fages camped at the little stream they christened Rio San Benito. Benedictines, or members of the order, were among the earliest monks, dating from the 6th century, and an important influence of the earliest medieval European orders.

The interior and entrance to the Monastery Room around 1934 display modern-era furniture and an electric fixture. The building itself, left standing since its construction, had suffered earthquake damage, and much of its original materials would still be used in the final restorations of 1949 financed by the Hearst Foundation.

At the rear of Mission San Juan Bautista's Monastery Room, a framed portrait of George Washington is displayed with a mix of dated furniture. Presidents of the United States always played important although infrequent roles in mission history, including the 1865 proclamation by President Lincoln emancipating mission properties and returning title patents to the Franciscan clergy.

This view through the archway at Mission San Juan Bautista of the Gen. Jose Castro House on the Mission Plaza in San Juan Bautista State Historic Park dates from around 1934. The California State Park Commission acquired the authentic plaza and surrounding buildings in 1935.

The old Zanetta House fountain is viewed from the west porch looking northwest towards Mission San Juan Bautista in San Juan Bautista State Historic Park. Many people settled in the new town after Mexico's war of independence from Spain, as private ownership titles were granted with the new secular laws.

Mission President Father Lasuén chose the spot to honor St. John the Baptist, and Mission San Juan Bautista was consecrated on June 24, 1797. As Alta California's 15th mission, it was the second of four established in one year on El Camino Real; Mission del Gloriosisimo Patriarca San José founded three days before, and Mission San Miguel Arcángel one month later. The tall masonry stucco tower, pictured around 1932, was built in 1926 to replicate the wooden 1860s tower removed earlier. Tower footings had been in place from the early mission's design but not used by the original builders. (Author's collection.)

The Spanish square at Mission San Juan Bautista has been lined with authentic buildings since the 1840s, including a livery and the Zanetta and Castro houses. California State Parks supervises the park and maintains it today. (Author's collection.)

The Mission San Juan Bautista is seen from the upper balcony of the Zanetta House on the town square. The town was located on a main route between the San Benito Mountain quicksilver mines, Hollister, Watsonville, Monterey, and Santa Cruz, serving as a primary staging, trade, and supply center over a wide area.

The earthen floor of the west cloister facing the church grounds has several doorways leading from the monastery or church. All the walls of old Mission San Juan Bautista were rebuilt and reinforced to avoid further earthquake damage.

A 200-year-old tradition at Mission San Juan Bautista, the Our Lady of Guadalupe image is enshrined near the altar of the mission. A witness to the miracle made famous the vision of a young girl recognized as the Virgin Mary as she appeared for several days before a man in 1531 near Mexico City. (Author's Collection)

A new rectory was completed in 1932 and then added as part of the early restoration to the buildings at Mission San Juan Bautista. By 1950, the mission walls had been completed using reinforced concrete for safety along with many original materials.

A picturesque vintage postcard view from around 1970 features rose blooms framing the mission arcade. Recent repairs to the walls are complete, and the luster of its beauty has materialized from restoration of this historic building.

The west loggia cloister facing the church grounds shows obvious separation of adobe bricks, with damage in the foreground and the apparent need for modern repairs. All Mission San Juan Bautista walls would be rebuilt and reinforced under the supervision of Harry Downie, master restorer of the missions of Monterey.

The Mission San Juan Bautista buildings are grand in stature and impressive even by today's architectural standards. The native population worshipping at the church peaked at 1,200 in 1823. Mission life required families to be remarried in the church to live together, and neophyte youths were housed in segregated barracks.

The southwest side of the mission church is seen here around 1934. Fathers Jose Manuel de Martiarena and Pedro Martinez supervised building the original church and found the native people friendly and cooperative. Mission San Juan Bautista included an adobe church, a monastery, a granary, barracks, guardhouses, and adobe houses for neophytes. By 1800, there were over 500 Indians living at the mission.

Old Mission San Juan Bautista has had unbroken successive pastors since its founding in 1797. This kept many of the mission buildings in good condition, although damaged from many tremors over the years. The original El Camino Real was changed by Father Lasuén to run directly to the side of mission property.

Mission San Juan Bautista's active serving Franciscan father, Estévan Tapis, was mission president for nine years after succeeding Father Lasuén and, by 1815, was assigned to Mission San Juan Bautista, where he died in 1825. Talented and musically inclined, Father Tapis assembled and conducted a native Indian choir known throughout the region. He is the only Franciscan given the exceptional honor of burial beneath the church floor at the mission.

Populations of natives would come from the east, including distant San Joaquin Valley's Sierra Miwoks and Yokuts. An expansive plan imagined by the friars to build missions reaching into the eastern foothills left many smaller estancia and *asistencia* (substation mission) chapels throughout California during peak mission years. (Author's collection.)

A c. 1934 Historic American Building Survey photograph depicts the south aisle door through a three-foot wall. Many overhead doorway lintels were traditionally carved stone to reinforce the structure.

These words over the door's transom greet visitors: *Hic domus Dei est & porta coeli* (this is the house of God and the doorway to Heaven). An inscription in gold lettering invites the visitor to observe that "this is the largest of the old churches built in three aisles." The church was enlarged after the arrival of Fr. Felipe del Arroyo de la Cuesta in 1808. His mastery of native languages brought recognition for his published works translating Mutsun grammar. (Author's collection.)

Pictured around 1934, the pastor's rectory had been added two years earlier on adjacent property from an old adobe rebuilt to accommodate the pastor's living quarters.

An expatriated carpenter, Thomas Doak from Boston was reported to have been the first US citizen to settle permanently in Spanish California. He built neophyte homes, the town square, and the mission while staying there until 1831. The wooden tower was built in a later period during the 1860s.

The northern side of the mission is pictured around 1934 and after the damage from the 1906 San Francisco Earthquake, showing several of the exposed walled-in archways in the interior. The mission had been affected like other sites along the San Andreas Fault.

This view of the mission grounds shows gardens surrounding the expansive footprint of the monastery building around 1934. To the left is the church, the largest of its kind in California. It was started in 1803 and, despite damage from numerous earthquakes, has been in continuous service since its beginning on July 1, 1812.

At the west end of the monastery around 1934, the mission grounds were often used for large church gatherings. The church became a backdrop to meetings enjoyed in the frequently pleasant outdoor weather.

A vintage postcard shows old Mission San Juan Bautista and the framed wood tower from the 1860s without its steeple top, later replaced by a framed stucco masonry tower. This, too, would be changed to today's *espadaña* design and relocated to the southeast corner. The new tower includes an original bell from the earliest of nine bells formerly used on wooden scaffolding. Two mission bells were recovered from a small chapel in San Francisco after the 1906 earthquake and used within the new bell tower's pierced openings.

This postcard view from prior to 1926 includes the New England–style tower that appeared out of context to many historians and history buffs. Once the mission had been restored in 1926, it became a premier destination to explore California's rich beauty and history.

In this photograph, Mission San Juan Bautista reflects a pervading serenity over its long history. The mission was built directly on the San Andreas Fault, and severe damage caused exterior walls of the church to collapse but left the enclosed nave untouched. The mission was fully restored by 1976.

The view through the mission arcade at California's only remaining Spanish town square features authentic buildings, including a livery stable to the right of the Zanetta house and landmarks from early San Juan Bautista. The mission was affected by the earliest days of secularization, becoming an early center of commerce in California. Mission acres had included a granary, barracks, a monastery, and adobe houses.

Each mission established pueblos or large quadrangles surrounding the community. Renovations to the church and to buildings facing the town square were completed in 1976, and California State Parks acquired the adjacent property to preserve its early Spanish heritage, as this mission's setting was the only remaining one of its kind.

Mission San Juan Bautista continues to be studied by scholars, architects, designers, and historians for the effects of settlement and history lurking within its walls. This measured drawing stored at the Library of Congress guided mission restoration and was used on projects during the CCC period.

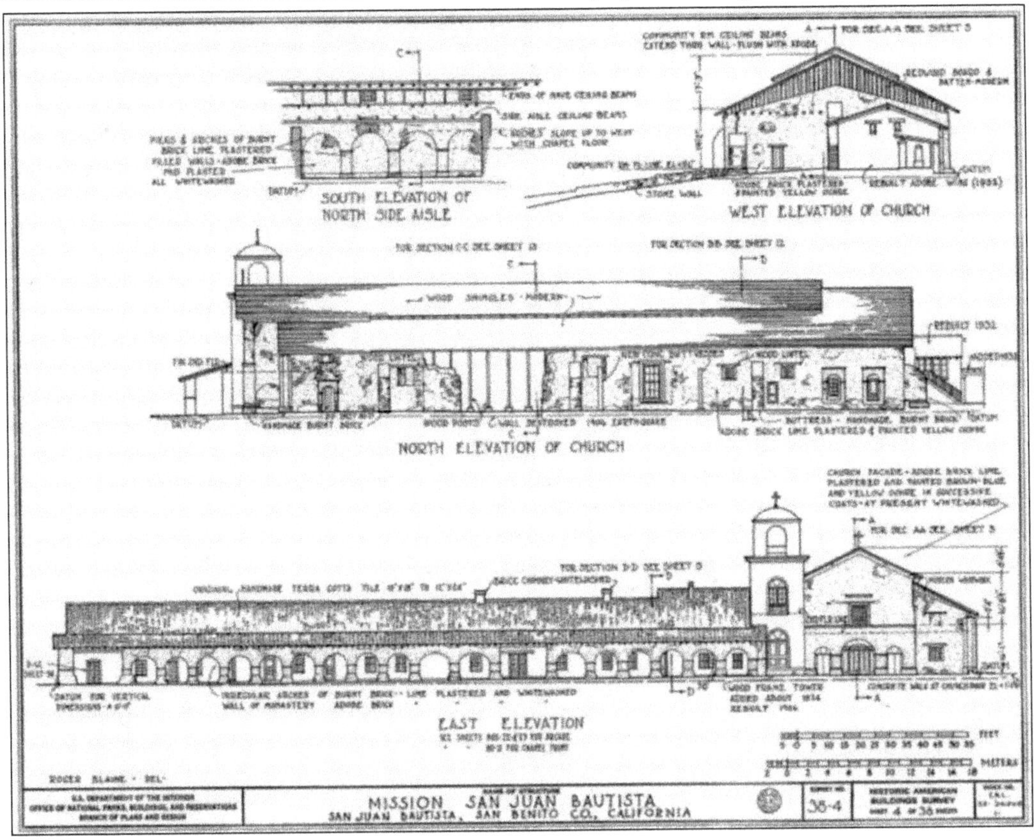

Six

Missions Past and Present

Touring El Camino Real

In 1771, Mission San Carlos Borromeo del Río Carmelo was founded by Fr. Junípero Serra on the banks of the Carmel River. It is the site of Carmel Mission Basilica in the verdant Carmel Valley chosen by Father Serra. Visit the museum store or e-mail store@carmelmission.org or call 831-624-1271 for touring information.

Father Serra named Mission San Antonio de Padua in 1771 for a favorite saint, Anthony of Padua, who died in 1231. The first mission was built from adobe on the banks of the San Antonio River among live oaks near the town of Jolon. After a drought, a later adobe and burned-brick mission with tile roofing was built in 1810 over a mile from the original near San Miguel Creek. It is often considered the best preserved of all the early missions, with a walking tour viewing ruins and archeological sites. The olive tree to the side of the mission church has stood for well over a century, and grapevines growing in the courtyard are from the original era. There is always a feeling of reverence and reward visiting this beautiful destination. The gift shop, docent tours, and retreats are available. Visit at Mission Creek Road in Jolon, call 831-385-4478, or go to www.missionsanantonio.net. (Author's collection.)

A founding friar, Fr. Buenaventura Sitjar was a highly skilled engineer who built 12 miles of aqueducts that bring water from a source four to five miles away to the mission property. By funneling water with special tiles to irrigate the fields and fill a stone-lined millpond and raceway, he fed the mission population, a tannery, and the livestock and turned old millstones for the granary before watering the adjacent wheat fields and orchards. (Author's collection.)

Mission Nuestra Señora de la Soledad, founded in 1791 by Fr. Fermín Lasuén, was located within the flood plain of the Salinas River Valley. It remains a peaceful place away from development and open to visitors as a fully restored mission. Take the Soledad exit near Highway 101 to 36641 Fort Romie Road, Soledad, or call 831-678-2586. (Author's collection.)

The chapel was fully restored in 1955 after having been stripped of all its existing adobe brick and archeological remains. Restorations made to the Mission Nuestra Señora de la Soledad were supervised by Harry Downie of Carmel, a master craftsman and restorer of Mission San Carlos Borromeo del Río Carmelo. (Author's collection.)

San Carlos Cathedral is seen in 2005 before renovations to the street entrance. Major earthquake safety upgrades have been made to the building, and it was rededicated in 2009. The restored church and grounds now feature a museum with many fascinating relics of history and may be visited at www.sancarloscathedral.org, or call 831-373-2628. (Author's collection.)

San Carlos Cathedral was dedicated in 1794 and had been built to replace Monterey's first Mission San Carlos Borromeo del Puerto de Monterey after its relocation in 1771 to Carmel by Father Serra. The stone facade emulates classic Spanish design, although it was constructed by the same builder of the uniquely proportioned Moorish-style Mission San Carlos Borromeo del Río Carmelo. The church is known as the Royal Presidio Chapel (La Capilla Real) and today is referred locally as San Carlos Cathedral. (Author's collection.)

The 200-foot-long arcade leads to the grand church, gardens, and statuary at Mission San Juan Bautista. The town square overlooks a dramatic view of the fertile San Benito River valley. (Author's collection.)

Founded on June 24, 1797, by Fr. Fermín Lasuén, Mission San Juan Bautista served a large population of mission Indians during its first six years. After 1806 and the arrival of Fr. Felipe de Arroyo de la Cuesta, a multilinguist who studied the Indian culture and language, the mission church was greatly expanded from the original 1803 structure. Today, this is the largest and most beautiful of all missions set within an authentic Spanish town square and a part of the California State Parks system. Old Mission San Juan Bautista is at 406 Second Street, San Juan Bautista (call 831-623-4528 or visit the website at www.oldmissionsjb.org). (Author's collection.)

Mission San Juan Bautista today stands completely restored with its new *espadaña* bell tower. California State Parks is the caretaker of the historic grounds and surrounding properties. (Author's collection.)

Fr. Junípero Serra and explorer Gaspar de Portolá founded Monterey and the presidio in June 1770. A gift to the city by Jane L. Stanford in 1891, the statue is at the second Monterey presidio, named El Castillo, and commemorates the padre's eternal blessing, standing over Monterey's harbor above the spot of their meeting on the day of its founding. (Author's collection.)

El Camino Real trail reached all the Spanish missions in Alta California to form a chain separated by a day's journey. The earliest paths of El Camino Real between Guatemala and Mexico covered thousand of miles and were developed by missionaries from Baja coming to Alta California. Father Serra dreamed of mission colonies settling Alta California, and the chain grew to include 21 main missions, substation missions, and estancias extending throughout Alta California's territories.

Bibliography

Berger, John A. *Franciscan Missions of California*. New York: G.P. Putnam's Sons, 1941.
Chapman, Charles E. *A History of California: The Spanish Period*. New York: Macmillan, 1921.
Elder, Paul. *The Old Spanish Missions of California: An Historical and Descriptive Sketch*. San Francisco: Paul Elder, 1913.
Fink, Augusta. *Monterey: The Presence of the Past*. San Francisco: Chronicle Books, 1972.
Gudde, Erwin G. *1000 California Place Names: Their Origin and Meaning*. Berkeley: University of California Press, 1965.
Hogan, Elizabeth L. *The California Missions*. Menlo Park, CA: Lane Publishing, 1989.
Hoover, Mildred Brooke, Hero Eugene Rensch, and Ethel Grace. *Historic Spots in California*. Stanford, CA: Stanford University Press, 1953.
Kimbro, Edna E., and Julia G. Costello with Tevvy Ball. *The California Missions: History, Art, and Preservation*. Los Angeles: J. Paul Getty Museum, 2009.
Mornin, Edward and Lorna. *Saints of California: A Guide to Places and Their Patrons*. Los Angeles: J. Paul Getty Museum, 2009.
Watkins, Major Rolin C. *History of Monterey and Santa Cruz Counties, California*. Vol. 1. Chicago: S.J. Clarke Publishing, 1925.
Wright, Ralph B., ed. *California's Missions*. Los Angeles: Sterling Press, 1950.